In the Embrace *of* Divine Melodies
CREATIVE BREATHS OF A SUFI SAINT

A Compilation of Ninety-Nine Utterances
by Shaykh Muhammad Hisham Kabbani

Preface by Dr. Ali Hussain

Institute for Spiritual & Cultural Advancement

Copyright 2020 Institute for Spiritual and Cultural Advancement.

All rights reserved. No part of this book may be reproduced, stored in a retrieval system, or transmitted in any form, or by any means, electronic, mechanical, photocopying, or otherwise, without the written permission of the Institute for Spiritual and Cultural Advancement (ISCA).

First Edition July 2020
ISBN: 978-1-938058-59-2
Printed in the United States of America.

Library of Congress Cataloging-in-Publication Data

TBD

Published and Distributed by:
Institute for Spiritual and Cultural Advancement
17195 Silver Parkway, #401
Fenton, MI 48430 USA
Tel: (888) 278-6624
Fax:(810) 815-0518
Email: info@sufilive.com
Web: http://www.sufilive.com

Author, Shaykh Muhammad Hisham Kabbani. Dhul Hijjah 2020.

Contents

A Lover's Preface	ix
Muhammad ﷺ: A Poem of Love	xiii
Introduction	xvii
Spiritual Stations	
One	1
Two	3
Three	5
Four	7
Five	9
Six	11
Seven	13
Eight	15
Nine	17
Ten	19
Eleven	21
Twelve	23
Thirteen	27
Fourteen	29
Fifteen	31
Sixteen	33
Seventeen	35
Eighteen	37
Nineteen	39
Twenty	41
Twenty-One	43
Twenty-Two	45
Twenty-Three	47
Twenty-Four	49
Twenty-Five	51
Twenty-Six	53
Twenty-Seven	55
Twenty-Eight	57
Twenty-Nine	59
Thirty	61
Thirty-One	63
Thirty-Two	65
Thirty-Three	69

Thirty-Four	71
Thirty-Five	73
Thirty-Six	75
Thirty-Seven	79
Thirty-Eight	81
Thirty-Nine	83
Forty	85
Forty-One	87
Forty-Two	89
Forty-Three	91
Forty-Four	93
Forty-Five	95
Forty-Six	97
Forty-Seven	99
Forty-Eight	101
Forty-Nine	103
Fifty	105
Fifty-One	107
Fifty-Two	109
Fifty-Three	111
Fifty-Four	113
Fifty-Five	115
Fifty-Six	117
Fifty-Seven	119
Fifty-Eight	121
Fifty-Nine	123
Sixty	125
Sixty-One	127
Sixty-Two	129
Sixty-Three	131
Sixty-Four	133
Sixty-Five	135
Sixty-Six	137
Sixty-Seven	139
Sixty-Eight	141
Sixty-Nine	143
Seventy	145
Seventy-One	147
Seventy-Two	149
Seventy-Three	151
Seventy-Four	153

Seventy-Five	155
Seventy-Six	157
Seventy-Seven	159
Seventy-Eight	161
Seventy-Nine	163
Eighty	165
Eighty-One	167
Eighty-Two	169
Eighty-Three	171
Eighty-Four	173
Eighty-Five	175
Eighty-Six	177
Eighty-Seven	179
Eighty-Eight	181
Eighty-Nine	183
Ninety	185
Ninety-One	187
Ninety-Two	189
Ninety-Three	191
Ninety-Four	193
Ninety-Five	195
Ninety-Six	197
Ninety-Seven	199
Ninety-Eight	201
Ninety-Nine	203

A LOVER'S PREFACE

> "Spirituality is all art, and art is all spirituality. You need *dhawq* (good taste) in order to belong in a *tariqa* (spiritual path), just as you need good taste to appreciate good art."

These are the powerful words of my Sufi guide, Mawlana Shaykh Hisham Kabbani. This was his response when I asked for his grace and permission to speak at an event about the marriage of art and spirituality in Islam. And it is this quote that exemplifies the spirit of meaning animating the life of this book: the teachings of a contemporary Sufi guide, who is connected with an unbroken chain of light, divine knowledge and love, to the most supreme expression of Divine Love and Creativity, the Master of Masters, our Prophet Muhammad ﷺ.

I have had the indescribable honor and blessing to accompany Mawlana Shaykh Hisham, in this physical world, for five years. Although, I am certain this short time, equal to a cosmic blink in the grand scheme of things, is furnished with an eternal covenant and immortal memory, when I was entrusted to his love and guidance in the world of spirits.

The most drastic transformation that I have gone through and experienced during these five years is the expansive journey into the heart of art and creativity which Mawlana Shaykh Hisham has opened for me, through his love.

As a creative writer and aspiring musician, I found myself on a path of *tazkiya* (self-purification) unlike any other: the indulgence in art and creativity not as a hobby, or even a career, but a spiritual vocation and the very channel through which my Sufi guide communicated to me his teachings.

I realized immediately that this ability to teach spirituality and esoteric realities of love and the cosmos through art and creativity is a high rank among the saints, because it requires that the guide and teacher is not only an 'artist of the soul', but also a perfected work of divine art. This is perhaps one of the most apt descriptions of Mawlana Shaykh Hisham.

In order to share some zephyrs of these creative

breaths from my guide, Mawlana Shaykh Hisham, I present you our beloved readers with this book: "In the Embrace of Divine Melodies: Creative Breaths of a Sufi Saint," a collection of 99 utterances on art, creativity and spirituality.

I hope that you can, and myself with you, receive the fragrance of these breaths directly into our hearts, whence they can bloom into endless love in color, melody and word.

We, the lovers and disciples of Mawlana Shaykh Hisham Kabbani, may God preserve his life and health, have compiled these utterances and present them here in a universal language that is relevant and understandable by people of all ages, ethnicities and religious backgrounds.

This motivation has encouraged us to translate terms like 'Allah' to God, Rasoolullah to the Prophet, and also leave honorary titles, such as ﷺ (*salla Allahu 'alayhi wa sallam* [May God send Benedictions upon him]), ﷺ (*'alayhi 's-salaam* [Peace be upon him]), ﷺ (*radiya Allahu 'anhu* [May God be pleased with him]) or ق (*qaddasa Allah sirruhu* [May God sanctify his secret]) as abbreviations.

We have also intentionally only numbered each of these reflections without a title, with the hope that each reader can name each saintly musing with what is inspired to their hearts as they delve into this ocean of creative breaths emanating from Mawlana Shaykh Hisham's sacred heart.

I pray that this book will bring the love of Mawlana Shaykh Hisham into the hearts of countless human beings and all life in this universe. We also hope that this effort brings the contentment of God, His Beloved Prophet Muhammad ﷺ, our Sufi guide Mawlana Shaykh Hisham, Mawlana Shaykh Nazim al-Haqqani, Mawlana Shaykh Abdullah al-Daghestani and all the saints in the illustrious Naqshbandi Golden Chain.

Ali Hussain, PhD
15 July, 2020
Fenton, Michigan

MUHAMMAD ﷺ: A POEM OF LOVE
BY SHAYKH HISHAM KABBANI

His birth in this world is the birth of Islam
But his Light was the first to be created
And from this Light is the birth of all Creation
He was and he is still The Prophet of all prophets
The Beacon of the Universe and Paradises
The Ocean of Beauty and Majesty
The Sky of Happiness and Love
He is The Perfect Servant of Allah ﷻ
He is The Servant
He is The Jewel, he is The Gem
He is The Mirror of the Reflections of The Divine
That brings the Light of Heavens on this dark earth
He is the one who is with everyone
As God said, "Know that the Prophet is within you."
He is the one that will intercede for humanity
He is the one that can stand in front of Allah ﷻ
by Allah's Permission
He is The Means for All Creation
He is The Intercessor for All Creations
He is The Light,
The one God dresses with Light upon Light!

He is The Illumination that Illuminates the Universe
His Secrets are in Heavens
His Secrets are in the Presence
His Secrets are in the Divine
His Secrets are like an abundant river
His Secrets dominate the creation because he is
Muhammad, the Messenger of God ﷺ!
He is the one that has been brought to Nearness
The Nearness that no nearness can reach
The Nearness where it was revealed to him
what he was asking for
The Nearness Gabriel was unable to reach
The Nearness of all nearnesses and that
no one can understand
His level, no one can understand
His level, no one can reach
His level, neither angel
nor human nor jinn can understand
He is what he is, only His Lord knows who he is
And as for us, we say:
He is The Jewel of jewels
Light of lights, Secret of secrets
Heaven of heavens, The Door to the Divine

The Way to every seeker,
The Struggle of every gnostic
He is the one Allah created
as Mercy for humanity
He is The Mercy and The Mercy is He
He is The Gifted Mercy
He is The Undescribed Mercy
He is The Joy, and oh, rejoice O Human Beings
in that mercy of his!
Allah ﷻ gave him what He did not give anyone else
Dressed him with what he did not dress anyone else
Loved him with what He did not love anyone else
He is Love!

INTRODUCTION

This is a spiritual book that will open the secrets of the Ninety-Nine Divine Names and Attributes for the reader. Everyone should buy ten copies, as every deed receives ten rewards!

For every station there are ten stations, so Station Number One is like Station Number Ten:

> *In Martial Arts, is there no discipline?*
> *It is full of discipline!*
> *In that Chinese or Japanese Martial Art,*
> *even if he, the Master, closes his eyes,*
> *he can feel who is coming from here,*
> *or here, or here.*
> *So, what do you think,*
> *if you are on the Way of God,*
> *can you not see*
> *right, left or from behind?*

Of course, you can see. Day and night, they will bring the reflection of the words and numbers to you, even to your bed!

Look at this carpet: when we first got it, it was the same color as that other carpet. However, over time and through people praying on it, it turned into a different shade of red. May God Almighty turn your hearts into a colored power! Red, in color and numbers, means success. They will give you a reward of ten colors! To achieve this, you need to only reflect and contemplate.

All of us here are studying, through our hearts, the meanings of the Ninety-Nine Divine Names, which reflect and appear in the heart of the Saint. This whole universe comes from the secret of these Names!

If you receive the Prophet Muhammad's ﷺ private names, your heart will be opened to the Ninety-Nine Divine Names. These Names will then consider you as their student; even if you are a Saint, they will look at you as a disciplined scholar.

Saints carry the secret of the Prophet ﷺ, so the secret of the Ninety-Nine Names come to their hearts depending on how much they achieve.

Shaykh Muhammad Hisham Kabbani
3 Dhul Hijjah 1441
24 July 2020
Fenton, Michigan

SPIRITUAL STATIONS

ONE

Just as Holy Verses
are engraved upon wood,
there will be engravings
of Divine Manifestations
with the Lights of the Prophet ﷺ,
because he is the one
who carries the Secrets
of Holy Verses.

TWO

Poetry is a tool
in the hands of Sufi Poets;
they use it to drink
from the Spring
of Divine Knowledge.

THREE

Poetry is the banner
of all Sufi Shaykhs,
and the beginning
of the beginning for them,
the Cup of Love
containing
all Secrets and Lights.

FOUR

Such love the poets had
in their hearts,
which they expressed in poetry
for us to understand
and replicate them,
to know that your heart
can open Secrets to you!

FIVE

These odes move people
who are full of vibrations,
vibrations of those who wrote them,
of the reciters,
and the singers who sing
in a nice melody.

SIX

When you listen to poetry and music,
you will begin to have a response from your body
and a reflection of your feelings
that make you to work together with that poetry
in order to invoke the Beloved One
that you feel you love.

SEVEN

That is why we say:

Invoking the Beloved ﷺ can be done

through poetry and music,

because it shows the feelings of people

and teaches them how to invoke their Lord.

EIGHT

Music gives you a way to feel happy.
Masters give you a way to believe in yourself.
When you have that experience,
you will overcome your fear,
and when fear is overcome,
there will be no more problems!

NINE

An art gallery shows art in different ways.
It appeals to the eyes, because it is nice.
Everything wild, disgusting and ugly
does not appeal to the eye.
How then are we going to meet our Lord?
With sweetness or with ugliness?

TEN

In Martial Arts, is there no discipline?
It is full of discipline!
In that Chinese or Japanese Martial Art,
even if he, the Master, closes his eyes,
he can feel who is coming from here,
or here, or here.
So, what do you think,
if you are on the Way of God,
can you not see
right, left or from behind?

ELEVEN

Art is all spirituality
and spirituality is all art;
you need good taste
to be on a Spiritual Path
as you do
in order to appreciate good art.

TWELVE

In the old Persian times,

a king made a competition

between two big artists, and said:

"The one who will draw the best artwork

will get this and this and this rewards from me."

The one on the right side

had a huge wall to draw on.

The one on the left side

also had a huge wall.

The king gave them each six months to do it.

One of them was drawing,

drawing very nicely, working hard,

and the other one was working hard

in scrubbing, polishing,

polishing the wall!

Between them was a curtain

so they could not see each other.

When time had arrived,

the sultan came and said:

"Show me your work!"

The second artist said:

"Let the one on the left
show you his artwork first;
I will show you mine after."
So they opened the curtain
and the artist showed his drawing
to the sultan.
When he finished looking,
he turned around and saw
the same artwork
reflected on the other wall
from the first one!
One was tired working day and night
and the other was clever,
polishing the wall to become a mirror.
In the mirror, it reflected everything!
The sultan did not know what to do.
The same artwork, the same design,
the same, nice artwork.
So he gave them both rewards.
The one who worked hard
had a nice picture that had been reflected
on the mirror of the other one,
who was working hard

to polish the wall.
So, polishing the heart
will reflect all kinds of Realities!
There is no obstacle in front of the heart;
there is nothing more to block
the Vision of Realities!

THIRTEEN

Look how the Prophet ﷺ cares
for everyone and everything.
Inanimate objects,
they are not even living,
and yet the Prophet ﷺ cares for them!
That is out of love.
When someone makes a piece of art,
he loves that piece of art.
So, the Prophet ﷺ wants a relationship
with everyone.
"And know that Muhammad ﷺ is in you!"

FOURTEEN

From Holy Qur'an, nothing will be left
except calligraphy, artwork.
Today, people are interested
in calligraphy of the Qur'an,
and there are some whose hearts are open
to learn about the Qur'an!

FIFTEEN

God said, "He honored human beings!"
by engraving them with His Beauty,
like an Artist.
If you go to an art gallery in New York
and see hundreds of different paintings,
can you say in front
of the one who painted it,
"This is ugly"?
You cannot say it,
as you will humiliate him,
and humiliation
is not allowed in any religion.
Rather, humility is taught
in every religion.

SIXTEEN

If we reject anyone from God's Servants,
who are Appearances
from His Beautiful Names and Attributes,
then we are trying to
find faults in The Engraver,
The One who carved and engraved us.
Artists do very nice sculptures,
very fine artwork.
You cannot come and say,
"I reject! This is bad!"
If you cannot do this for an artist in this world,
how can you reject these Appearances
that have appeared?
Then you are coming against The One who
produced, molded, sculpted and designed them!

SEVENTEEN

The Prophet ﷺ said,
"There will be nothing left of the Holy Qur'an
except its calligraphy,"
which is the heart of the Holy Qur'an!
Not only to draw it,
but also to understand its sweetness
through its Holy Verses.
That is the real calligraphy!

EIGHTEEN

Every Saint is identified by a color.
This is a Heavenly Light
that a Saint is dressed in,
which every moment
becomes stronger and stronger.

NINETEEN

If you take the red color
and put it under a huge microscope,
how many colors do you see?
Only one red color?
You will see an infinite number
of colors of red
under the microscope,
the yellow, the black, the green,
all different colors!
There is no one color the same.
Do you think that God
has only seven colors in the rainbow?
Or are there colors
that we are never able to see?
There are infinite colors
the eyes cannot see,
even the spiritual eyes cannot see!

TWENTY

God is *al-Badi`*, The Innovator.
He does what no one can do.
Saints are like that,
taking from God's *ibda,*
from The Name *al-Badi`,*
The One who fashions,
The One who fashions things
in a way that is appealing to everyone.
If you have a garden of roses
that are the same color,
it might be appealing once or twice,
but not more.
It must be mixed of different colors
in order to be appealing.
Saints are fashioned and woven in a way that
they are harmonious with each other.
So, when you look at them,
you see that coordination.
and that gives you happiness,
to see them together.

TWENTY-ONE

Let us consider
that this world is black and white,
no color.
You will see that
there is no creativity in it;
there is not that word,
"Magnificence" in Arabic.
God makes things harmonious.
If a movie is black and white,
you do not want to see it,
because there is no color.
Look here:
Everyone has different clothes,
different dress,
and everything is harmonious,
like when you dress,
you try to wear matching clothes.
You say, "This one is not matching,"
and you throw it away,
or, "Matching or not, I will wear it!"
or, "No, don't wear it, it is not matching!"

If someone does not know what he is wearing,
how can he know the hearts of people?

TWENTY-TWO

Look, when winter comes
the whole trees become no leaves,
only branches of one color,
like black and white.
All these branches here,
what color do they have?
Grey,
between white and black.
You cannot see any more beauty,
but when Spring comes,
He gives life and gives death!

TWENTY-THREE

All of us,
we are to our Guide
like different flowers.
Every flower has its own nice smell,
like different jewels.
Every jewel likes its own color,
and The Guide is happy
to see all these colors and flowers.

TWENTY-FOUR

Saints have different badges with different colors;
they look at the colors and go through them.
They go in with angels
who open different ways for them.
Every Saint has a color
and cannot go beyond that color;
they are known by their colors.
Their bodies are no longer forms.
They are subtle
and can be seen right through!

TWENTY-FIVE

As the Prophet ﷺ mentioned,

in Paradise you see through Heavenly Creation,

as their beauty makes them transparent.

They are not thick and dense.

There, there is nothing with a veil;

you can see through them

and see different colors.

These colors cannot be compared

to a rainbow.

Here, people see a rainbow

and think it is magnificent

So, Saints have different colors,

which means different bridges

and tunnels to the Prophet ﷺ.

TWENTY-SIX

Depending on your color
you have a seat with the Prophet ﷺ.
That seat is also made transparent
by the same color you have.
You cannot reside on a different color!

TWENTY-SEVEN

In the eyes of the Prophet ﷺ
all his Companions are the same.
If they saw him day and night,
they are his Companions.
If they saw him only once
and believed in him,
still, they are his Companions.
There is no change in their title,
but God may dress one of them in black
another in blue and this one in red.
Everyone has a different color.
God gave them a different garment,
but it is all a Heavenly Dress.

TWENTY-EIGHT

Shah Naqshband ق said:
"Everything changed!"
His Guide had dressed him
with the Garment of Knowledge
and different dresses of Gnosticism.
About these, he said:
"As my Guide
was putting his head over my head
and dressed me,
I saw these different dresses
coming from different colors,
Heavenly Dresses coming above me.
And as they came,
the doors of my heart were opened
for Divine Knowledge.
I would have never been able to learn these
through studying!"

TWENTY-NINE

Our mission is to meet everyone
and take grace from everyone.
What is the issue?
Then, we will become like a rainbow
with many colors,
which is better than being only one color!
However,
usually you prefer one color.
So keep that and add more to it,
as it was said:
"This robe has many colors."
Likewise, a disciple can have many colors.

THIRTY

You look at the trees
and you like the one full of colors,
like in the autumn season:
The trees have red, yellow and orange leaves.
You look at another tree, which is only green.
Which one takes your eyes more?
The one with the many colors.
The green one is not as colorful,
although green is nice.
You will have both from Saints;
you will have green within the colorful one!
Whereas scholars have one, the green one,
Saints have both.
In this way, you will become
a rainbow of worship!

THIRTY-ONE

You see:

Our Muhammad ﷺ came to unify people;

he did not come to separate them,

but he came to integrate them.

Look at the color red.

Look at it!

It is nice.

Now, how many colors can it make?

Red with other colors

can make many more colors,

pink, purple…

These colors and many others,

put them together and what happens?

You get a rainbow of colors

that everyone likes to look at.

Woven together, these colors come from one womb,

from our Master Muhammad ﷺ!
God said:

"Know that the Messenger is within you!"

If he is in us, then how?

In that Light!

THIRTY-TWO

A rainbow is made of how many colors?
How many colors can you count?
They are seven.
When you look at a rainbow,
you see the red, blue, green and yellow.
Have you seen the rainbow?
In reality, when you look at it
you see some colors
and you can count them,
but not everything
that your eyes see is reality.
Human beings are limited;
they cannot see.
That is why we ask
about Heavenly Divine Knowledge,
because our eyes are limited;
the eyes cannot see except a rainbow,
and only rarely.
If we can see
but cannot differentiate
these seven colors,

then we are mistaken.
If you take a magnifier
and take the red color,
you will see
it consists of infinite reds.
You cannot describe to people
these colors.
When you say "red",
everyone understands,
and when you say "pink",
everyone also understands.
But this red is like the sun;
when you see it,
you think you see yellow.
Bring a prism,
put it in a sunray.
What do you see?
Different colors.
This means that God
is giving us time in this world.
Not everything that we cannot accept,
we reject.
Your eyes cannot see Reality.

We cannot see,

we are blind,

all of us,

every one of us!

Each is depending on his level.

THIRTY-THREE

Ask for Heavenly Lights!
Do not ask for these colors
that people now are fighting about
and seeking to change it.
They think there are better colors.
No! You must ask for Heavenly Lights,
to shine!
Try to reach those Lights.
Our colors are not important,
but rather what God is dressing
on your creation from Heavenly Lights,
that is important!

THIRTY-FOUR

If there were holes in the ceiling,
you could see beams of sunlight
coming inside this room,
shining on everyone.
And if that light was coming
through a hole like a prism,
you could see different colors,
and everyone
would have their own color.
People would say,
"I have red."
"I have blue."
"I have green."

THIRTY-FIVE

We have seven main colors,
but in reality
every color has its own
infinite number of colors,
because every color
is changing slightly
and making millions of colors.
If you take the walls away,
what will happen?
All of us
would be under one color.
There is only one Light,
not two, three, four or ten.
That is The One, True Source!
If we can zoom inside our heart
like healers zoom inside their own hearts
and send rays to heal people from their fears,
then we can overcome our fears and illnesses!
There is not a single illness
that has no cure.

THIRTY-SIX

God said in Holy Qur'an:
"O Children of Adam!
Wear your beautiful apparel
at every time and place of prayer."
"O human Beings!"
speaking to the Muslims
but also, all human beings;
He is addressing everyone,
inviting them to enter Beauty:
"Take your ornaments,
the things you are proud of,
take them to every mosque;
take those things you look great with.
Do not go empty-handed!"
If God is ordering us
to take our ornament,
the best of what we have
to the masjid,
like people say,
"I am going to the museum."
To do what?

Why do you go to the museum?
To see all the artwork
that makes that place a museum.
God is telling us,
for people of this world:
They take their ornaments with them
to their buildings,
and that makes the building a museum.
What do you think of taking the best
of what you have to the mosque?
Do you see a museum
hanging its pictures on the floor?
No, only on high places;
they are hanging it high!
The artists consider it lively.
So consider what God said
in the Holy Qur'an:
"Take your ornaments,
do not leave your mosques empty
of God's Beautiful Names and Attributes
and Holy Verses.
These Beautiful Names and Attributes
will be manifested while written on the wall

or hanging in frames.

THIRTY-SEVEN

It is an honor to be among you,
because if not for you
I will speak to whom?
So I need you,
and that is why I am here!
Because everyone
is a flower to our Guide,
everyone is a different color,
a different taste of honey
that bees take from the flower,
and each one
is dear to our dear Guide,
God bless his soul!

THIRTY-EIGHT

God gave us a way
through our Guide
to get different colored diamonds
from the heart of Prophet ﷺ.
Why? Because God said:
"We have given you a lot!"
and "plenty" never finishes;
to the Greatness of God,
"plenty" is nothing,
it is minimal.
It means,
"plenty" has no limits!

THIRTY-NINE

When God put the Light of Muhammad ﷺ

in our Master Adam's ﷺ forehead,

it became decorated with different lights.

When we decorate with different lights,

it makes people happy;

they forget about themselves,

they dance, move and listen to music.

Where is it coming from?

From the Light on Adam's ﷺ forehead,

all Heavens were shining

with different rainbows of colors!

Angels were dancing with Heavenly, Divine Music!

FORTY

The devil saw this Light

as a rainbow coming

from the forehead of Adam ﷺ.

If we take one color from the rainbow,

red for instance,

and look at it through a prism,

we will see

infinite numbers of red.

It means:

What we are seeing is not reality.

It is not just one color,

it is an infinite number of colors,

each one lighter than the other!

A fountain of beautiful colors was coming

from the Beauty and Light

from our Master Adam ﷺ.

God said:

"I took a handful of My Light and said,

'Be Muhammad!'"

Can you describe

the beauty of that Light?

We cannot.
What we are describing,
you can only speak on the tongue,
but Saints go further,
not just by the tongue
but vision as well;
they can see what happened
when the devil did not prostrate.
They can see in the past
and in the future.
Do not underestimate
the power of Saints,
especially their Sultan!

FORTY-ONE

Do not bring up people's faults!
Let them conceal their faults
and try to see them
and benefit
from following the right way
that suits them.
Here, everyone
is wearing different styles
and colors of dress,
and according to the Verse,
everyone has different decorations.
For everyone
there is a direction
to their goal.
So, let us strive together
towards all that is good!

FORTY-TWO

"The Prophet ﷺ is a jewel,"

a jewel with many colors,

a rainbow of colors!

Do you know rainbows?

How many colors?

Seven.

Is it really only seven?

How many colors?

There are infinite colors!

Because, any of these seven colors,

if you magnify them,

it gives more and more,

like a universe.

May God give us His Grace

from the Prophet ﷺ,

the happiness

to be happy

in this world and the Next.

What you need to do

is to praise the Prophet ﷺ!

FORTY-THREE

Every action that comes from us
has a color.
Saints see if you have the right color,
and for that action,
God replaces His punishment
with forgiveness.
He will not punish you,
He will forgive you!
We cannot see that, but Saints can.

FORTY-FOUR

Our Guide said that his Guide
passed him one spoon.
And each bowl has a different taste,
all from the same pot,
but the one that the Grandmaster
passes to our Guide
had a different taste.
He said:
"Nothing has sweetness
like that bowl from Grandmaster."
It was lentils,
it had oil and vinegar.
So how could it be sweet?
But he said:
"It was sweeter than honey!"
He took the first spoon,
but when he took the second spoon,
it was sweeter than the first!
When he took the third spoon,
it was sweeter than the second!
When he took the fourth spoon,

he could see lights
coming from that spoon,
and a different taste
coming from each light!
So, he has four spoons,
each with four colors
and each color
has a different taste.
The fifth spoon had eight colors
and each color had a different taste
and full of knowledge!

FORTY-FIVE

You know these laser lights
that people like to go and see?
Imagine!
These are colors of this world.
What about the colors of Paradise?

FORTY-SIX

One time,
I was passing by the window
of Grandmaster's room,
going to a Session of Remembrance,
and there was a window.
My oneself was telling me to look
and another was telling me to not look.
These things,
sometimes you cannot control.
If you do not look,
you miss the opportunity.
So, I looked.
I saw Grandmaster
sitting and opening his mouth.
You know,
on cold days when you go out
and you blow air,
you see fog coming out.
I was shocked to see what was coming out
from his mouth: Light!
From his mouth a white color

and from his head a greenish color!
It was coming up
and they were mixing like a rainbow.
The whole ceiling had disappeared
and you could see it going up
through this universe
until you could no longer see it!

FORTY-SEVEN

Grandmaster passed by a garden and said:
"Regardless of how much
you are going to give it of water,
you will not make it turn green;
the only thing that will make it green,
which means 'pure',
is Divine Remembrance!"
Those Circles of Remembrance
that we sit in
are a garden that never gets yellow;
it is always green.
This example means,
to transform yourself
and become a "green person".
Our Master Khidr ﷺ
is the "Green Man",
because wherever he passed,
it became green.
That is why he is called, "Khidr".

FORTY-EIGHT

The Prophet ﷺ is ascending.
Do you think the Ascension stopped?
Knowledge never stops.
So, the Prophet ﷺ is ascending
in his knowledge more and more.
Do you think there is only one
station of "Two Bows Length or Nearer"?
Look at the rainbow.
How many colors does it have?
Seven.
But if you take one color
like red, and look at it
under a microscope,
you will see
infinite hues of red
or infinite fields of black,
all of them different.
The Prophet ﷺ is always
in Two Bows Length or Nearer;
he is always
moving without end,

like the horizon:

When you reach one,

there is another.

He is in a continuous ascension!

FORTY-NINE

When you go to the ocean
what do you see?
What is the color of the ocean?
Do you see anything else?
To see more
you need to dive into the ocean,
then you will see
how everything completely changes
into a colorful scenery,
and you will begin to witness nature's beauty
as you have never witnessed on earth!

FIFTY

Pilgrimage is like a rainbow
which has different faces of colors,
which gives you a different taste.
If you look with a magnifier,
you see many more colors
that make you happy.
Also, Pilgrimage is like a rainbow
showing different Manifestations
of God's Beautiful Names and Attributes.
So each year you get more manifestations
than the year before,
all the way from the time of the Prophet ﷺ
until the year you go
for your Pilgrimage.

FIFTY-ONE

Thank you very much
for honoring us
by being here tonight
with all these beautiful faces,
like many flowers in a garden.
When you have a garden
with flowers of only one color,
after one hour you get bored,
but when you have
different colors,
you want to keep looking!
May God forgive all of us.

FIFTY-TWO

"Decorate your hearts
and your mosques
with the Holy Qur'an."
It will stay there!
God will give it a color
through His Angels;
He will order the angels
to go to the reciters of the Qur'an
and gift them a color
for their recitation.

FIFTY-THREE

He wants to give
Manifestations of Heavens:
One comes, the other goes,
and each is different in color,
but first,
you have to get The Key!

FIFTY-FOUR

There are knowledges
that people are unable to study.
Their mind becomes very rigid.
When you look into a rainbow,
how many colors do you see?
They say there are seven,
but when you look deeper
there are an infinite number of colors:
reds, yellows, greens, blues and violets
and every color is repeated infinitely!
Therefore, it is not what your eye can see,
but what your heart sees!

FIFTY-FIVE

Today reciters are not any more reciting
in a melodious voice.
I ask you:
Did anyone hear the Qur'an
from the Prophet ﷺ?
No one heard.
What we heard are the voices
of normal people.
Who heard from the Prophet ﷺ?
What kind of voice
do you think the Prophet ﷺ had?
What kind of voice compares
to the voice of his Companions?
What do you think about the Prophet ﷺ?
They heard his voice,
and what kind of voice did they hear?
All of them heard the same voice.
God gave everyone a certain way
of hearing the voice
of our Master Muhammad ﷺ.

His voice is like a rainbow
that changed with the audience!

FIFTY-SIX

What do you think is the sweetness
that the Prophet ﷺ heard?
The Mercy of the Qur'an is so sweet!
When you want mercy for someone,
you give the best to them.
Do not think that
when you read the Qur'an
you are understanding
or carrying its sweetness.
God is Most Merciful
and He will change our voice
to beautiful sounds.
These are the ones we have to hear.

FIFTY-SEVEN

We believe in reciting odes.
I care for them
and like people to be happy,
and I like them
to be taught how to sing.
Some have good voices,
but do not have a melody,
singing in a haphazard way,
one from the east,
one from the west,
one from the north,
and up and down.
The way of recitation
is very important.

FIFTY-EIGHT

Once our Master Moses ﷺ

was traveling in a desert

and came to a huge mountain

from where he heard

a beautiful, melodious voice

coming from a cave.

He was instantly attracted to it.

As he approached,

the voice grew louder and clearer.

Then he heard someone

repeatedly reciting:

"Praise to God,

the One Who has favored me

over many,

whom He previously favored.

He favored me more!"

FIFTY-NINE

Today they recite
and that is okay,
but in the time of the Prophet ﷺ,
they were reciting
in melody.
From whom did they hear it?
From the Prophet ﷺ!
If he did not do it,
they would not do it.
So the Companions heard
the recitation of the Prophet ﷺ.
All heard
the recitation of ancestors.
I am speaking physically,
not spiritually.
So what we hear now
is maybe
the minimum of its beauty.

SIXTY

Sometimes you have a key
that opens the lock,
sometimes they give you many keys
and they say:
"Open the door."
It is your luck.
If you get the right key,
it opens;
if you do not get the right key,
it is closed.
Any stringed instrument has
many different strings.
If you touch one string,
a sound comes,
if you touch another,
another sound comes,
all different sounds.
From one to another,
it changes.
You might like one,
but you do not like the other.

God has given us a "string";
He gave a "key" for everyone.
So you cannot say:
"This one has a key
and this one does not."
God is Just;
when He gives,
He gives to everyone!

SIXTY-ONE

The Mother of the Believers,

A'isha ﷺ said:

"Whoever wants to hear

the sound of *al-Kawthar*,

then let them

put their fingers in their ears;

they will hear the waves

and the water flowing!"

Put them inside.

Do you hear it?

We used to do that

when we were young.

SIXTY-TWO

This Remembrance will be
circling the Throne.
All of it comes together,
connects together
and makes a sound like bees.

SIXTY-THREE

The power that angels are using
to carry that worship
cannot be counted in circles;
it can only be counted
by Heavenly Circles,
which are billions of movements.
Because when you say "*Allah*!"
that sound that came
from your mouth
will go all the way
to the Day of Judgement!
Physics teaches us
that when the sound
"*Allah*" comes,
it also creates
a smaller circle of sound
until it covers
all circles by reaching Heavens!

SIXTY-FOUR

The Prophet ﷺ said:
"When God invited me
to 'Two Bows Length or Nearer,'
He made every word I spoke
an Ocean of Knowledge."
God created a Paradise,
especially for the words
of the Prophet ﷺ,
in his heart.
Words spoken
without letters and sound!
The Prophet (s) was understanding
with letters without sound
and words with sound
without sound.
God was revealing to his heart
without writing
and the Prophet ﷺ was understanding
what God was sending to him!

SIXTY-FIVE

What kind of

Heavenly Musical Sound

did the Prophet ﷺ hear

from Gabriel ﷺ,

and what sound

was the Prophet ﷺ hearing

after he went

to "Two Bows Length or Nearer"?

SIXTY-SIX

In absolute calm
golden stars glowed
with the luminescence of pearls,
and for each pearl
50,000 angels whirled
in a lake of galaxies
making a Heavenly Sound
that resembled the singing
of one million birds together
with a million bees.
Everything was moving
at the speed of light,
but at the same time
everything
was silent and calm.

SIXTY-SEVEN

Hearing with your eardrum
can detect
more than a seismograph
that detects the slightest
tremor of earthquakes
deep inside the earth!
The sound goes on the eardrum
and beats like
Al-Zahra Ensemble
and their musical drumbeats!

SIXTY-EIGHT

Sound does not stop.

If we say,

"*Muhammad ﷺ!*"

that sound wave,

that magnetic wave

will continue.

So you say,

"*Muhammad ﷺ!*"

and the wave continues to say,

"*Muhammad ﷺ, Muhammad ﷺ,*

Muhammad ﷺ, Muhammad ﷺ...!"

That is like an echo

and that echo

of the name Muhammad ﷺ

will never stop;

it will continue reciting

until the Day of Judgment!

SIXTY-NINE

One day after the dawn prayer,

our Master ʿAbdul-Khaliq al-Ghujdawani ق,

with his honor and greatness

that God dressed him with,

was resting,

and a majestic voice said:

"Oh ʿAbdul-Khaliq!

By order, go to that rock in the city

and wait for the order

coming from Heaven."

He was hearing the voice of an angel.

When you say,

"*Laa ilaaha illa-Llah,*"

if your heart is open,

you will hear that sound,

a Heavenly Sound that

you will be more than astonished;

you will melt from its sweetness,

from the sound of that angel!

When you say,

"*Laa ilaaha illa-Llah,*"

God will keep creating angels
and you will be melting,
like the melting of ice,
how it disappears and becomes water.
If you put it back in the fridge,
its previous form returns.
So you will disappear
without a form;
as much as you melt your ego,
you will disappear,
ending up with an angelic form!

SEVENTY

One person here now
was reciting odes in one place,
As the earth moves around the sun,
this ode will never stop,
because sound never stops;
it is composed of waves
that are moving.
If I say here, "*Allah!*"
it continues moving all the way
to the people back there
because of the microphone system,
but God has a Heavenly Microphone.
Their Heavenly Microphone
will keep saying, "*Allah, Allah!*"
from here to no end,
because the Prophet ﷺ mentioned:
"When the angels see a group of people
praising God, they join them
and make Remembrance with them."
And this never stops
until the Day of Judgment!

SEVENTY-ONE

Who heard the Holy Spirit
bringing Divine Revelation
to the Prophet ﷺ?
Who heard that voice
other than Prophet ﷺ?
No one.
What was that angelic sound
that came with that Verse?
What was that sweetness?
What was sacred
behind that Verse?
Who heard it
other than the Prophet ﷺ?
Is it like our talk
or when we memorize the Holy Qur'an?
Or is it something special
for the Prophet ﷺ
that is beyond our minds?
What kind of sweetness came
with that Verse of Holy Qur'an?

Who heard from the Prophet ﷺ?

SEVENTY-TWO

The instrument is repentance,
but how do you do it?
You know the flute,
it has holes.
If you cover one hole,
one sound comes out.
Cover another hole,
another sound comes out.
So we need such an instrument
that indicates where or where not
to put our finger
so that it makes a beautiful sound.
As much as you say,
"*Astaghfirullah, may God forgive us!*"
the angels hear and taste it
and take it to the Divine Presence,
especially in Ramadan.
If you say, "*Astaghfirullah*" again,
it will have another taste
that the Saints feel from their followers
whom they present to the Prophet ﷺ

along with the beautiful sound

of their repentance.

SEVENTY-THREE

"Thunder" is an angel
as big as the thumb.
It has a whip.
When he hits the cloud,
he moves it.
He is responsible for the cloud.
He is so small,
but when he hits
he can hit the cloud.
God wants to show that this small angel
can make such a sound
by hitting the cloud.
God is praising Himself by Himself!
Who created that small angel
called "Thunder"?
He is so small
yet he is praising his Lord!
God gave him that power
to hit the clouds with his whip.

SEVENTY-FOUR

The moment
the two index fingers touch one other,
they make a sound
that does not stop
until the Day of Judgement.
God gave some people the understanding
of what has been sent as a Message.
Now, they have iCloud.
Before, the Saints were using
The Beautiful Divine Names
to reach humanity.
So that Mercy God gave to Saints,
when they disperse it to the disciples,
everyone will get a share.
When you take
whatever they give you of Mercy,
it must be in right proportion
in order to click together.

SEVENTY-FIVE

You have to be careful,
to look at your breath
in and out
and not to be heedless
for a moment.
You have to bring
all your power
and concentrate it in your heart
with all these powers
from different parts of the body.
Through meditation,
we begin to hear them all
making Remembrance.
Our life is Divine Remembrance;
every cell in our body
is Remembrance.
Look at the heart.
What is it saying?
"Huuuu! Huuuu!"
Listen to it.
God made every organ to say

His Names and Attributes;

every organ has

a different Heavenly Musical Sound.

If you watch yourself well,

you will see that,

and if you do not,

you will not see it.

You must gather all your power

to know the Secret of your appearance.

SEVENTY-SIX

Each one of us indicates
there is a Creator,
as no two people are alike.
If an artist were to make
a sketch of human beings
his drawings would be limited,
but if you look at human beings,
you will soon realize
there are six billion people
in the world,
each with an entirely
different shape and image!

SEVENTY-SEVEN

Artists draw nice pictures of nature.
You see them with their big canvas
and all their brushes,
looking into nature
and drawing pictures.
If an artist draws a picture,
you look at the picture
and you look at nature,
saying, "Very nice!"
They may come to you and ask:
"You want the picture
or you want the real one?"
Of course we say:
"Give us the real!"
Paradise for the laypeople
is a duplicate of the real one
that has the reality in it.
The one that has the picture in it
has a picture of the reality,
but you cannot have the pleasure
you get from the real nature.

You get some pleasure

by looking at it,

but in the real one

you can eat the fruits,

drink the water

and do whatever you like!

SEVENTY-EIGHT

God showed the beauty
of the World of Beauty.
When it is opened
they see beauty in everything,
not only on earth, but in the universe!
And when they reach it,
they cannot look
at anything else but that beauty!
People here say:
"There are competitions in the arts."
Who is the best artist?
From their drawings
you can see this artist is better
than that one.
When Saints see the beauty
of what God created,
they can no longer see
that anything is not beautiful.
They are attracted
to the beauty that God
put in earth and in Heavens!

SEVENTY-NINE

An artist will have something
inside of him;
he has an artistic touch.
So what will he do?
He will draw a beautiful calligraphy.
Look, all these big calligraphers
of the Holy Qur'an:
They want to show
all their beauty for the Holy Qur'an,
they want to show their best
for God's Word.
From time of the Prophet ﷺ until today
they created different styles
to show the beauty of the Holy Qur'an
through their love,
because there must be something
in them that makes them do that.
Not everyone can do that.
People who love flowers
put flowers together to make a bouquet.
Everyone has a different ambition

or touch or taste!
When you have that,
you must put all of that
to what you want to do.

EIGHTY

If human beings have
this artistic touch,
they like to express
their artistic feelings
in something that stands out.
God created arts and artistic touches.
This whole universe
that He created
is all like a beautiful appearance,
a beautiful manifestation
of His Name "The Creator".
When God wanted to show His Beauty,
He created the Essence
of the Reality of our Master Muhammad ﷺ
before any creation!

EIGHTY-ONE

What happens in Spring?
The rain comes
and everything becomes alive.
Similarly, if anyone says
"*Muḥammad*!"
his heart comes alive,
as he is the Spring of This Universe,
he is the Spring of Heavens,
he is the Spring of Every Lover.
The evidence is that
God ordered the angels
to send benedictions on him,
because he is the Spring,
he is the Beautiful One
whom angels are in need
to look at in order
to take power from him.
You look at a picture and say,
"This is a nice picture
drawn by a nice artist.
I hope something is alive

in the picture,"
because the picture is nice.
What do you think
about the heart of a Saint?
The Holy Qur'an has mentioned
the heart ninety-seven times,
which means,
the heart is important!

EIGHTY-TWO

Do you want Paradise?
Of course!
Everyone wants Paradise,
or else why would they come here
from far away to see lovely
beautiful people?
This is a garden of flowers
with different colors;
everyone is different.
You cannot see anyone the same,
which is God's Power
that everyone has different features.
An artist draws many copies
of the same thing,
but God does not need to copy.
He can create everyone
with different features.

EIGHTY-THREE

Today, they write the Qur'an
very beautifully,
but the people do not know
how to read the Verses;
they just come and say,
"This is very beautiful!"
What is left of the Holy Qur'an?
Artists' drawings.
Is there anything else?
When you mention the Qur'an
to non-Muslims,
they immediately think of calligraphy.
At least they are interested in it,
which is good.

EIGHTY-FOUR

You may see that
trees have a chain of prophets:
The Prophet ﷺ
is in the middle
and the other prophets
are all around.
Many artists make this
in beautiful calligraphy.

EIGHTY-FIVE

Music takes you up;

it is a spiritual access.

These musicians

are being honorably

and heavenly supported

because they make

everyone happy!

EIGHTY-SIX

There was a famous musician
at a Gathering of Remembrance.
He said:
"When I play music with my singers,
we can bring 100,000 people together,
but if it rains like this
no one will stay.
I am amazed at how these people
are mesmerized, not moving,
sending benedictions on the Prophet ﷺ
while the water is pouring!"

EIGHTY-SEVEN

There was one poet
who wanted to praise the king
in order to be known
that he is a good poet.
The king listened and said:
"I heard this before."
The poet said, "But I wrote it!"
The king called another man and said:
"You! Do you know it?"
He said, "Yes," and read it word for word.
Then the king called another man
and asked him, "Do you know it?"
He said, "Yes," and read it word for word.
He then brought another
who also recited it the same.
The poet said, "No, I wrote it!"
These poets were like
a photocopy machine.
Saints have students
that are like mirrors;
they immediately reflect

their knowledge in the heart
of their students.
These are rare students
and they are true reflections
of the Master's teachings.

EIGHTY-EIGHT

The tongue is helpless
and speechless,
it cannot express
what is inside the heart.
The poet tries to express
and writes poetry,
but there is another poetry
that works on the heart.
That is how Saints
attract people to them!

EIGHTY-NINE

We are coming to God
through the Beloved One,
the one whom the tongue
of every poet
was frozen to speak of
and trembling to describe.
No one can describe him
except God!

NINETY

If we take all of this
from our hearts,
when we are invoking,
we are going to hear the answer.
It is not important
to reflect our feelings
when we write poetry.
It is nice,
but we need to continue
until we get a response!
And what is the response?
It is an inspiration,
a revelation through your heart!

NINETY-ONE

Every person
whose heart is full of love
will become
a fountain of poetry.
God will inspire his heart
to write poetry!

NINETY-TWO

Divine Love
can only be known
through tasting,
and the Saints put
that taste of love
in their followers.
It is something
that comes spontaneously
without preparation,
like poets who have
a pen in their hand,
and write spontaneously
without preparation.
May God guide us
to that spontaneous,
Heavenly Knowledge.

NINETY-THREE

Saints give hope
to your soul and spirit.
Without that hope
we feel cut.
That is why most poetry
is based on love,
because the best hope
is to have someone to love
who also loves you.
For God to show us that love
is important.
He called our Master Muhammad ﷺ
His Beloved.
Our Master Muhammad ﷺ
is the Beloved One.
God created our Master Muhammad ﷺ
with His Love.

NINETY-FOUR

Abdul Aziz ad-Dahlawi ق,
a great guide in India,
was reciting poetry and saying:
"Whatever the Guide orders, do it!
Even if he says to paint your prayer rug
with wine."
In Arabic poetry
"wine" is love.
Although, he did not explain it this way.
He is saying metaphorically,
"Pray, even on a rug that is painted with love,
as it will take you to the Divine Presence!"
This means:
"Be drunk in God's Love
and come into prayer
where there is nothing but Him!"

NINETY-FIVE

In the past,

before memorizing the Qur'an,

they used to memorize all kinds of poetry

of love for the Prophet ﷺ!

Then, when they became 12 years of age,

they began to teach spirituality.

Now, we do not see that!

NINETY-SIX

Everything shows our level of love for it,
in poetry, in verses, in reading the Qur'an
or Prophetic Speech.
The vibrations have a tone of that love,
so the mind and heart can understand it
and respond.
As much as you force your mind
to drop the body and look for the spirit,
these vibrations will become
like angelic movements
that are accepted
and loved by God and His Prophet ﷺ.

NINETY-SEVEN

Whatever descriptions poets write,
they are only swimming in a valley,
unable to aptly express
the Greatness of the Prophet ﷺ.
Although it is acceptable,
how deep can we reach to his Reality?
We would have to dive into
one ocean after another
to reach the Greatness
of our Master Muhammad ﷺ!

NINETY-EIGHT

In one line of poetry
you can put a whole book!
That is why people must know
that there is something hidden
in every person,
something that he wants
and she wants to hold
in order to climb
and move upwards.
Or, they can move in any direction
in order to satisfy their needs.

NINETY-NINE

Each station has its ocean,
like poetry.
When you write poetry,
you come to a hidden place
called "The Ocean of Trusts,"
and everyone will get that.
It is an ocean of wonders;
the Saints are going around
in that ocean
to be granted their power.
When they pass through it,
their power is taken
and when they get out,
their power is restored
to be distributed to their brothers.
That level we are speaking of now
has meaning,
but if you go one level higher,
you cannot understand
what we are saying,
which is why the Saints

hide the power
of this spiritual station
from their disciples.

www.ingramcontent.com/pod-product-compliance
Lightning Source LLC
Chambersburg PA
CBHW030149100526
44592CB00009B/192